30 Ways to Start Your Business, Get It in Order, and Increase Your Net Worth without Working Harder

30 Ways to Start Your Business, Get It in Order, and Increase Your Net Worth without Working Harder

Mary Baker

Copyright © 2013 by Mary Baker.

ISBN:	Softcover	978-1-4797-5964-4
	Ebook	978-1-4797-5965-1

All rights reserved. No part of this book may be reproduced or transmitted in any form or by any means, electronic or mechanical, including photocopying, recording, or by any information storage and retrieval system, without permission in writing from the copyright owner.

This book was printed in the United States of America.

To order additional copies of this book, contact:
Xlibris Corporation
1-888-795-4274
www.Xlibris.com
Orders@Xlibris.com
126158

Contents

If you're in business, you need this book! 11
Steps to Starting a Business 13
Getting Your Business in Order 35
Tips for Keeping More Money in Your Business by Saving on Taxes 55

About the Author 77

I would like to dedicate this book to Curtis, my husband and best friend, for his love and unselfish support of all my endeavors and for always being there for me. Also to Rajah and Walif, my sons that any parent would be proud of and thanks for teaching me while I was teaching you. A special note to my grandchildren for understanding that Grandmom is always here for you.

Take control of your business, and increase your net worth now!

—Mary Baker

If you're in business, you need this book!

Why every small-business owner, or anyone who is thinking about starting a business, need to read this book.

This book is for every small-business owner or anyone who is thinking about starting a business and does not know where to start. The reason I wrote this book is to educate entrepreneurs on how to run a business smoothly from the start without working harder later on. I had to learn how to run a business by trial and error, and believe me, it had an impact on my net worth. I am saving you the time and effort by sharing with you what I learned being a business owner.

I get entrepreneurs in my office every day complaining about their businesses and how they are not making the money they would like to make. I get entrepreneurs in my office who received notices from the Internal Revenue Service (IRS) and do not know what to do with them or just throw the notices in the garbage because they are frustrated with their business because it is not in order. This is bad. The major complaints I get from the IRS is that business owners just do not know how to start a business properly and keep it in order. If you start your business properly in the beginning, you will increase your business net worth in the end.

This book is the ABCs of running a successful business that you are not told or taught by anyone. Everyone teaches about how to run a business, but no one ever explains the simple steps on how to run a ***business***.

For example, most people tell you that to be successful, you need to manage your money, but no one teaches you how to balance your bank account. Well, this book teaches you the simple steps of running a successful business that must people are ashamed to ask or just do not think about when starting a business.

These simple steps will save you money in your business.

Steps to Starting a Business

1. Write a business plan. The first thing to do when you start a business is to form goals and objectives for your new company. A successful start to any business requires a detailed outline of what you plan to accomplish. One of the reasons having a business plan is important is that it will help you consider the details of your business and its future. As you are working on your plan, you will probably find that there are many aspects of your new business that you have not considered. Getting started with a business plan will help you save money and time since you will be able to deal with the issues before they become a problem.

Start small and dream big.

—Rich Dad

Action Step: Write down your goals and objectives for your business.

2. Select your business name. Chose a name that is right for your business, a name that will attract customers to your business. Research your business name to make sure it is available for you to use before applying for any legal documents for it. Businesses file names on a per-state basis, so other companies may be using the same or a similar name in other states. Conducting a trademark search ensures that your unique company name isn't already in use.

Be aggressive in getting media coverage.

—Liz Lange

Media coverage is free, which is a very attractive price tag for most small businesses. But media coverage is usually not an accident. You have to take it in your own hands to get coverage.

Action Step: Chose three names for your business.

3. Set up a legal business structure. Research or talk to a professional to determine which business structure is right for you. Forming a corporation or LLC can protect your personal assets from business debts. Additionally, incorporating can provide credibility and tax benefits. The business structure you chose will not only have an impact on your business assets but on personal assets as well, so make sure you structure your business accordingly.

If you do things well, do them better. Be daring, be first, be different, be just.

—Anita Roddick

Action Step: Decide on a legal structure for your business.

4. Obtain a employer identification number (EIN). Incorporated businesses and companies that hire employees must obtain an EIN. This number can be obtained from the federal government. Your business federal EIN is your social security number for your business. You should keep this number in a safe place because you will use it for all your business needs. When buying from or servicing to other companies, you will use this number, not your personal social security number. Your federal EIN is the start of your business; you are now a legal business.

> *Share your success and help others succeed. Give everyone a chance to have a piece of the pie. If the pie's not big enough, make a bigger pie.*
>
> —Dave Thomas

Action Step: Get a federal employer identification number for your business.

5. Satisfy the business license requirements. Most state, county, and local governments require businesses to obtain licenses before they begin to operate. You will need to contact the appropriate agencies to find out if your business needs additional licenses. It is very important to have the proper license before conducting any business to protect you from any lawsuit. If a license is required for your business, I say make a copy of it and carry it with you at all times when conducting business. If an opportunity comes your way, having the proper license will make you stand out from the crowd, letting the potential client know you are serious about your business.

Patience; this is the greatest business asset. Wait for the right time to make your moves.

—J. Paul Getty

Action Step: Get the proper licenses for your business.

6. Satisfy the insurance requirements. Incorporating or forming a corporation does not provide a company with business insurance. Most companies obtain general business insurance from an insurance provider. Corporations and LLCs that hire employees also typically obtain unemployment and workers compensation insurance. Protect your business and yourself by having insurance to cover you when something happens. Knowing you are protected gives you peace of mind and helps you focus more on your business and not on the problems.

When you reach an obstacle, turn it into an opportunity. You have the choice. You can overcome and be a winner, or you can allow it to overcome you and be a loser. The choice is yours and yours alone. Refuse to throw in the towel. Go that extra mile that failures refuse to travel. It is far better to be exhausted from success than to be rested from failure.

—Mary Kay Ash

Action Step: Get the proper insurance for your business.

7. Establish a business presence. Identify a location for the business, and establish a business address. If you are working outside of your home, the location of your business is very important. Consider your customers when choosing a location: is it easy to find or is there convenience in parking? If you are working from home, do you want your customers to know where you live or is your home set up to run your business properly?

> *Every brand isn't for everybody, and everybody isn't for every brand.*
>
> —Liz Lange

In other words, do what small businesses do best and focus on a niche—and then own that niche. Be at the top.

Action Step: Chose the location for your business.

8. Establish a web presence. Your business web presence is just as important as your business presence. Not having an effective website eliminates opportunities for new customers and more profit. With social media today, is your website built for customers to find you, old or new? Having a great web presence is very importance because this is how most people find a business in today's society.

> *The Web puts an exponential twist on the whole word of mouth thing, because word of mouth is now happening virally.*
>
> —Blue Man

The web is a megaphone. It gives you leverage and dramatically increases the spread of any talk about your business. The web makes it easier for word of mouth to spread, and spread more quickly and more widely.

Action Step: Create a website for your business.

9. Open a bank account and merchant account. To protect your corporate or LLC veil, you must maintain separate business and personal accounts and records. Establish a separate business bank account so that your personal assets are not comingled with business funds. Banks may also require an employer identification number (EIN) in order to open a business checking account. Having a bank account not only helps you in keeping your business in order, it also helps you to establish a relationship with your local bank. Having a relationship with your local bank is important as your business grows; you will see later how this will help your business when you need a loan.

> *The best thing a business owner can do is to establish a relationship with your local bank; you will need it services in the future.*
>
> —Mary Baker

Action Step: Open a bank account for your business.

10. Establish proper accounting procedures. The company corporation understands that paying your taxes is only part of the picture when it comes to setting up your business. Whether you need help setting up your chart of accounts, have questions about completing a specific tax form, or need answers to business questions, seek a professional. Request a thirty-minute consultation with a recommended professional to discuss your unique situation and get the answers you need.

> *Choose your accountant like you choose your spouse—make sure it is someone you can trust.*
>
> —Mary Baker

Action Step: Establish procedures for your business.

Get started. Schedule an opening day for your business, and you are on your way.

Getting Your Business in Order

The next steps to having a successful business are to make sure you have your business in order. When I say *order*, make sure you have every aspect of your business in some type of format so that you understand what is going on in your business at all times. In order to understand your business, you need to be involved in your business.

Listed below are things you need to have in order for your business to be successful.

11. Team. You will need a team of players who will make your business successful. By saying *players*, I mean staff, accountant, attorney, system people, etc., who will make your life easier by keeping your business running smoothly. It is very important to understand that you cannot do it by yourself and that you need help in running a successful business. When picking your team, make sure these are people you can work with and can follow instructions. The team you pick determines how successful your business will be.

> *You are a product of your environment. So choose the environment that will best develop you toward your objective. Analyze your life in terms of its environment. Are the things around you helping you towards success? Or are they holding you back?*
>
> —W. Clement Stone

Action Step: Pick a team.

12. Leadership. How you lead your team is very important. You want to be a role model. Learn from the experts, read their books, attend their seminars, and recognize your strengths. Your team is looking at how you value your business, and they will value your business the same way. Never let your team see you sweat; if there is a problem, handle it in a professional manner and move on to the next issue. Put your leadership plan in place and stick to it.

Do something. Either lead, follow, or get out of the way.

—Ted Turner

Action Step: Choose the type of leader you would like to be.

13. Delegate. Sell your strengths. Buy your weakness. It is better to contract out what you do not know and spend your time on the things you do know. Use the people in your team for what each one is best at, and this will keep your business in order. Using your team member on what they are good at not only gives a person fulfillment, it also help you keep loyal team members. Delegate. Delegate. Delegate.

Time is your most important resource.
You can do so much in ten minutes.
Ten minutes; once gone is gone for good.

—Ingvar Kamprad

Action Step: Decide on what person will do what on your team.

14. Be there. Know what is going on in your business at all times. This is very important because in order for your business to be in order, you need to know what is going on in the business. No one is going to care about your business like you will, and if you are not present, then why should anyone else be there? Having a presence in your business lets the staff know you care, and if someone is not working, you will know immediately, not when it is too late, like losing a customer. Be there and know what is going on with your business at all times.

> *Don't spend so much time trying to choose the perfect opportunity, that you miss the right opportunity.*
>
> —Michael Dell

Action Step: Decide on how you would like to be present in your business.

15. Invest in your business. Do not get complacent with your business and stop investing in it. For example, make sure your phone system, computers, and databases are up-to-date. Make sure you have everything you need to run your business properly. Never look at your business as an expense; always look at it as an investment. The more you put in, the more you get out. Invest in your business in the beginning; it will save you time in the end, and remember, your time should be spent on getting new customers.

You must remain focused on your journey to greatness.

—*Les Brown*

Action Step: Decide on what your business needs in the beginning to help it grow.

16. Follow up. How do you measure your business results? Write a business plan, put some targets someplace where you can see them, and graph your course. Are you on target with your plan, or are you off course from your plan? Do you really know? If you are not measuring up to your plan, find out why and make the necessary adjustments to get on course. You should have some type of measurable tool for your business so you know how your business is doing according to your plan.

If you can build a business up big enough, it's respectable.

—Will Rogers

Action Step: Check your business plan and see if you are hitting your targets.

17. Do your homework. Compare your products and services to the competition. How do you measure up? Find out what is working for your competition and do the same and more. Your products and services should always be outstanding compared to your competition. You should know what is going on in your industry at all times; by doing this, you will always be ahead. Knowing what is going on in your business helps you to keep your business in order.

> *We are all competing against mediocrity.*
>
> —Blue Man

Instead of focusing on the competition, strive for a higher level of creativity. To create a great business, create something extraordinary instead of falling into a rut and settling for average.

Action Step: Do some research and find out what your competitor is doing.

18. Plan your strategy. Do a survey to find out what your potential clients want, and fill their need. Do not assume you know what your consumers need and want; ask them what you can do for them. Do not sell; find out what they want to buy. Knowing what your customers want will save you time and money in the long run. By knowing now, you are focusing on the specific things they need and not investing in unnecessary things. Having a strategy helps you keep things in order because you know what you need to do.

> *You can't do today's job with yesterday's methods and be in business tomorrow.*
>
> —Author Unknown

Action Step: Survey your customers to find out what they want.

19. Build a strong and effective database. Know your target market and the people who are willing and can afford your product or service. Do research to find the right consumers for your product or service. Make sure you know how to reach your target market, and market to them on a constant basis. Utilize the web; gather lists of organizations and agencies who would benefit from your product or service. Gather customers' information and create a database that can be used for all your marketing—for the present and the future.

They say a year in the Internet business is like a dog year . . . equivalent to seven years in a regular person's life. In other words, it's evolving fast and faster.

—Vinton Cerf

Action Step: Decide on how you are going to collect information for your database.

20. Put an action plan in place. Use the SMART acronym: specific, measurable, achievable, realistic, and timely. Be specific about the product or service you are going to offer and what benefits it has. Make sure you have a plan for your product or service where you will be able to measure the progress on how you are doing. Do you need to change anything or keep everything the same? Create a goal that is achievable. When setting your goal, make sure it is realistic for your product or service, something that you know you will be able to achieve. Set a goal that is timely. Plan a goal you know you will be able to reach in a time period so that if changes need to be made, the business will still operate. When you are SMART about your business, you will always have order.

> *I like to tell people that all of our products and business will go through three phases. There's vision, patience, and execution.*
>
> —Steve Ballmer

Action Step: Plan. Plan. Plan.

Tips for Keeping More Money in Your Business by Saving on Taxes

21. Auto expenses. If you use your car for business, or your business owns its own vehicle, you can deduct some of the costs of keeping it on the road. Mastering the rules of car-expense deductions can be tricky but well worth your while.

There are two methods of claiming expenses:

- *Actual expense method.* You keep track of and deduct all of your actual business-related expenses.

- *Standard mileage rate method.* You deduct a certain amount (the standard mileage rate) for each mile driven, in addition to all business-related tolls and parking fees.

As a rule, if you use a newer car primarily for business, the actual expense method provides a larger deduction at tax time. If you use the actual expense method, you can also deduct depreciation on the vehicle. To qualify for the standard mileage rate, you must use it the first year you use a car for your business activity. Moreover, you can't use the standard mileage rate if you have claimed accelerated depreciation deductions in prior years or have taken a Section 179 deduction for the vehicle.

If your auto is used for both business and pleasure, only the business portion produces a tax deduction. That means you must keep track of how often you use the vehicle for business and add it all up at the end of the year. Certainly, if you own just one car or truck, no IRS auditor will let you get away with claiming that 100 percent of its use was related to your business.

> *Income tax returns are the most imaginative fiction being written today.*
>
> —Herman Wouk

Action Step: Get a logbook or software to track your business travels.

22. Expenses of going into business. Once you're running a business, expenses such as advertising, utilities, office supplies, and repairs can be deducted as current business expenses—but not before you open your doors for business. The costs of getting a business started are capital expenses, and you may deduct what the IRS allows the first year you're in business; any remainder must be deducted in equal amounts over the next fifteen years.

If you expect your business to make a profit immediately, you may be able to work around this rule by delaying paying some bills until after you're in business or by doing a small amount of business just to officially start. However, if, like many businesses, you will suffer losses during the first few years of operation, you might be better off taking the deduction over five years so that you'll have some profits to offset.

> *[The Internal Revenue Code is] about 10 times the size of the Bible and, unlike the Bible, contains no good news.*
>
> —Don Nickles

Action Step: Decide on what method you are going to use to keep track of your expenses.

23. Advertising and promotion materials. The cost of the ordinary advertising of your goods or services—business cards, yellow page ads, and so on—is deductible as a current expense. Promotional costs that create business goodwill—for example, sponsoring a peewee football team—are also deductible as long as there is a clear connection between the sponsorship and your business. For example, naming the team the Big Blues Restaurant or listing the business name in the program is evidence of the promotion effort.

> *This is too difficult for a mathematician. It takes a philosopher.*
>
> —Albert Einstein (on filing for tax returns)

Action Step: Decide on how much you are going to spend on your advertising and marketing materials.

24. Books and legal and professional fees. Business books, including those that help you do without legal and tax professionals, are fully deductible as a cost of doing business.

Fees that you pay to lawyers, tax professionals, or consultants generally can be deducted in the year incurred. However, if the work clearly relates to future years, they must be deducted over the life of the benefit you get from the lawyer or other professional.

> *The income tax created more criminals than any other single act of government.*
>
> —Barry Goldwater

Action Step: Keep records of all books and legal and professional fees. Remember that the more you learn, the more you can deduct.

25. Education expenses. You can deduct education expenses if they are related to your current business, trade, or occupation. The expense must be to maintain or improve skills required in your present employment. (The cost of education that qualifies you for a new job isn't deductible.)

There may be liberty and justice for all, but there are tax breaks only for some.

—Martin A. Sullivan

Action Step: Learn as much as you can. The more you learn, the more successful you become.

26. Travel. When you travel for business, you can deduct many expenses, including costs of plane fare, costs of operating your car, taxis fares, lodging, meals, shipping business materials, laundry, telephone calls, faxes, and tips.

However, if you take your family along, you can deduct only your own expenses.

> *Why does a slight tax increase cost you two hundred dollars and a substantial tax cut save you thirty cents?*
>
> —Peg Bracken

Action Step: Travel to your clients if you can. The happier the client, the better for your business and the more you can deduct.

27. Business entertaining. If you pick up the tab for entertaining present or prospective customers, you may deduct 50 percent of the cost if it is either

- directly related to the business and business is discussed at the event—for example, a catered meeting at your office; or

- associated with the business, and the entertainment takes place immediately before or after a business discussion.

Make notes. On the receipt or bill, always make a note of the specific business purpose—for example, "Lunch with Mary Smith of Smith Manufacturing Co. to discuss widget contract." The IRS will look for this.

> *Today, it takes more brains and effort to make out the income-tax form than it does to make the income.*
>
> —Alfred E. Neuman

Action Step: Entertain your clients to get more business. You can have fun and increase your net worth at the same time.

28. Bad debts. If someone stiffs your business, the bad debt may or may not be deductible—it depends on the kind of product your business sells.

- Goods—If your business sells goods, you can deduct the cost of goods that you sell but aren't paid for.

- Services—If, however, your business provides services, no deduction is allowed for the time you devoted to a client or customer who doesn't pay.

I didn't realize how hard it was to run a small business.

-Andrew Mason

Action Step: Keep records of all bad debts and remember not to do business with them again.

29. Interest. If you use credit to finance business purchases, the interest and carrying charges are fully tax-deductible. The same is true if you take out a personal loan and use the proceeds for your business. Be sure to keep good records demonstrating that the credit was used for the business.

> *The hardest thing in the world to understand is the income tax.*
>
> —Albert Einstein

Action Step: Credit is good for the business. Establish business credit so you do not have to use your personal credit.

30. Taxes. Taxes incurred in operating your business are generally deductible. How and when they are deducted depends on the type of tax:

- *Sales tax* on items you buy for your business's day-to-day operations is deductible as part of the cost of the items; it's not deducted separately. However, tax on a big business asset, such as a car, must be added to the car's cost basis; it isn't deductible entirely in the year the car was bought.

- *Excise and fuel taxes* are separately deductible expenses.

- If your business pays *employment taxes*, the employer's share is deductible as a business expense. Self-employment tax is paid by individuals, not their businesses, and so it isn't a business expense.

- *Federal income tax* paid on business income is never deductible. *State income tax* can be deducted on your federal return as an itemized deduction, not as a business expense.

- *Real estate tax* on property used for business is deductible, along with any special local assessments for repairs or maintenance. If the assessment is for an improvement—for example, to build a sidewalk—it isn't immediately deductible; instead, it is deducted over a period of years.

Action Step: Make sure you pay all your taxes. You have enough going on in your business; you do not need the tax authorizes down your back.

Mary Baker

It's simple: The more tax deductions your business can legitimately take, the lower its taxable profit will be. Also, in addition to *putting more money into your pocket* at the end of the year, the tax code provisions that govern deductions can also yield a personal benefit. It all depends on paying careful attention to IRS rules on just what is—and isn't—deductible.

When you're totaling up your business's expenses at the end of the year, don't overlook these important business tax deductions.

> *Accounting is the language of business.*
>
> —*Warren Buffet*

"Quite frankly . . . it's been brought to our attention that you still have a shirt on your back."

Remember, running a business in the beginning the proper way will increase your business net worth in the end.

Ask Mary Baker a business question at www.getyourbizinorder.com.

About the Author

Mary Baker is the founder of "Get Your Business In Order™" movement. My mission is to help entrepreneurs to get their business in order and increase their bottom line by transition their personal and business lives for a profitable company. It is my desire and mission to assist business owners in increasing the quality of their lives by reclaiming their business; in order to create awesome personal and professional lives, while living life on their own terms as entrepreneurs. I am passionate and dedicated to helping business owners to overcome the fear of owning a business, overcome their financial barriers and focus more on their business, and all the things that hinder them from living their dreams and owning a successful business. I want business owners to stop living under false pretense that their business is making the profit it should be making and start making the profit their companies should be making by getting their business in order.

It is about stepping out of the old way of doing things and doing business a new way increasing profit. It is about making financial decisions to achieve the dream you had about owning a business.

My goals is to encourage, motivate, teach and equip business owners to take that quantum leap to connect and implement the **3Ps (purpose, passion, profit)**; and have the business they dreamed to have.

Well, this thing is personal. I am sick and tired of seeing business owners paying thousands of dollars to the IRS and state during audits simply because they do not have their business paperwork in order. Oh yeah, must people say I will never get audit and if I do I will deal with it at that time. I said the same thing until I got audit. The audit was bad, simply because I did not have my paperwork in order or have simple things like copies of my receipts. After being audit, I was determined to educate business owners on how to keep their business in order and how to be prepared for an audit.

I have worked hard to educate myself on how to run a business and be prepared for an audit if it happens again and teach other about their business. I believe that everybody can own their own business if they work hard at it. I get pleasure out of helping other business owners to success in their business by teaching them how to get their business in order.

Currently, Mary owns three businesses, has authored one book, "Whatever Happened to Outstanding Customer Service?" A book promoting the important of customer service in all walks of life.

Mary has delivered financial literacy presentations at several non-profit organizations, hospitals and universities. Through her workshops, courses, coaching programs, and products, Mary teaches her clients how to balance their lives and finances to achieve successful businesses. Mary is the go to person to get your business in order without working harder, whether you are a new business owner or experience business owner. If your business needs a financial makeover Mary is the person to call.